Goldrich and Heisler

Songbook Volume 1

Lyrics by
Marcy Heisler

Music by
Zina Goldrich

ISBN 0-634-09377-0
Second Edition printed in December 2004
Printed in USA

Published by:
THE MARCY AND ZINA COMPANY
1382 Third Avenue, #343   New York, NY 10021
Visit our website at www.goldrichandheisler.com

Music Production: Anne Kaye, Kaye-Houston Music
Cover Design & Production: Julia Evins, Evins Design
Cover Photography: Beth Kelly
Production Manager: Linda Kiel, The Kielcom Group, Inc.
Web Site Design: Jennie Starr, www.jenniestarr.com

Acknowledgments

This book is dedicated with much love to our parents, Lois and Jerry Heisler, and Sybil and Jim Goldrich, who always help us to make our own party and sing our own song.

And to Zina's husband — and Marcy's dear friend — Aaron Stern...we couldn't have done this without you.

In addition, we would like to thank the following people and organizations for their generosity, encouragement, and inspiration:

Our families: Amy Goldrich, Robert Stern, Cynthia Stern, Tali Kaplan, David Stern, Eileen Heisler and Adam Wolman, and Kevin and Lynnette McCollum.

Our agent, Peter Hagan, and The Gersh Agency.

Our friends and mentors who offered their business and creative expertise: Maxyne Lang, Kevin McCollum, Jeffrey Seller, Michelle Pollack and The Producing Office, Michael Kerker (ASCAP), Ken Sandler, Charlie Shanian, Shari Simpson Cabelin, Susan Kim, David Friedman, Craig Coursey (Theatre Circle), Pat Cook, Jim Caruso, Ivor Clark, Emma Bailey, Loren Plotkin, Jeannette Chambers, Chris Burney, David Braun, Freddie Gershon, Tim McDonald, Music Theatre International, Eugene Gwozdz, Kurt Deutsch, Rick Starr (Hollywood Sheet Music), Rick Elice, Sarah Douglas and Charles Kopelman, and Maury Yeston, who provided us not only with a wonderful quote, but years of inspiration and guidance.

Special thanks to Scott Coulter, Matt Scharfglass, Christopher Sung, and all the other veterans of the Marcy and Zina shows who give their time and talent and make performing so much fun. Special thanks also to Kristin Chenoweth, Julia Murney, Paige Price, Becky Lillie, and the many other wonderful actors who put their own amazing spin on our work and make us learn new things every performance.

To the places and stages that gave us chances to grow, work, and learn, including The Ordway Center for the Performing Arts, Second Stage Theatre, The Walt Disney Company, Ars Nova Theatre, The King Kong Room, The Gardenia, Don't Tell Mama, Interlochen Center for the Arts, Northwoods Theatre Institute, Berkshire Theatre Festival — and the BMI Lehman Engel Musical Theatre workshop, where we met.

Marcy: Jennie Lipowich Starr, Jon Segal, Julie Kaufman, Patrice Gallagher, John Pollack, Tamar Schoenberg, Pam Winski, Shannon Barr, Jeff and Julia Lazarus, our fellow A-trainers, Devan Sipher, my Yalie boys, and the rest of my dear friends who make living in New York such a joy. I would also like to thank my grandparents, Sylvia and Joe Goldberg, and Anne and Harold Heisler...and my Aunt Sue, who took a seven-year old poet and her dreams very seriously. You are always here with me.

Special thanks to AB, AP, PD, FS, DS, GB, CS, MS, MW, JB, JG, and JR.

Zina: Jillian Jenkins, Robert and Beatrice Sherman, Edith Wax, Albin Knopka, Fran Sears and Bob Sann, Heidi and Robert Silverstone, Tammy and Steve Weinfeld, Abbi Rose and Michael Blum, Lisa and Steven Rizzi, and the rest of my wonderful friends. Special thanks to my grandparents, Ruth and Mike Ehrlich, for taking me to Broadway shows when I was a kid, and to Lucy and Ira Goldrich, and Zivel Niden, always in my heart.

Most of all, my love and gratitude to my husband, Aaron, who helps me dream big and make music every day. There are no words...And a big hug for our two most delicious creations, Rachel and Adam Stern.

Goldrich and Heisler

Songbook Volume 1

Contents

Apathetic Man

*Trio**

Lyrics by
MARCY HEISLER

Music by
ZINA GOLDRICH

*Can be done as a solo

af-ter some cha-blis, it's true, there was a long-ing glance or two while walk-ing through the vil-lage to my door. I had a

real nice time I said and soft-ly tilt-ed back my head and if he was sur-prised, he did-n't look it. I said

I don't usu-ally do this, but I've got some tea up-stairs, and he

gent-ly took my hand, and then he shook it.

6

8

Baltimore

Lyrics by
MARCY HEISLER

Music by
ZINA GOLDRICH

24

28

Beautiful You

Lyrics by
MARCY HEISLER

Music by
ZINA GOLDRICH

Boom Boom
Duet

Lyrics by
MARCY HEISLER

Music by
ZINA GOLDRICH

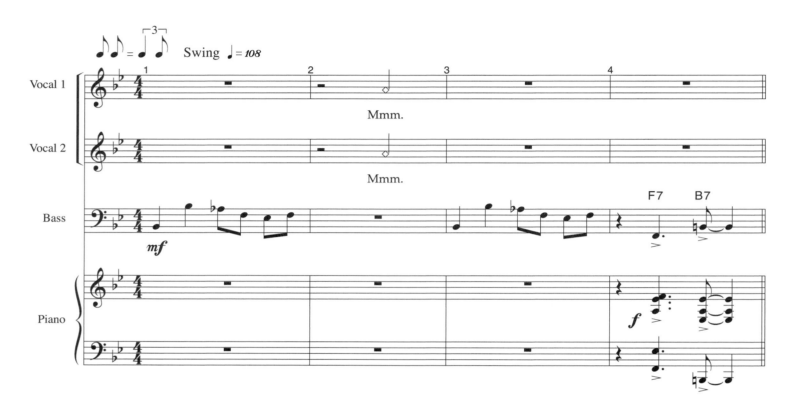

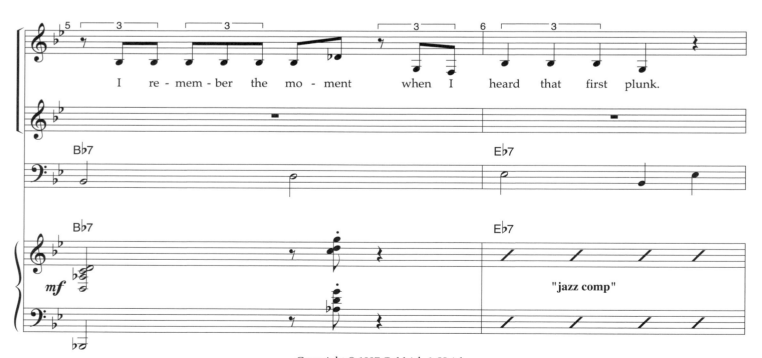

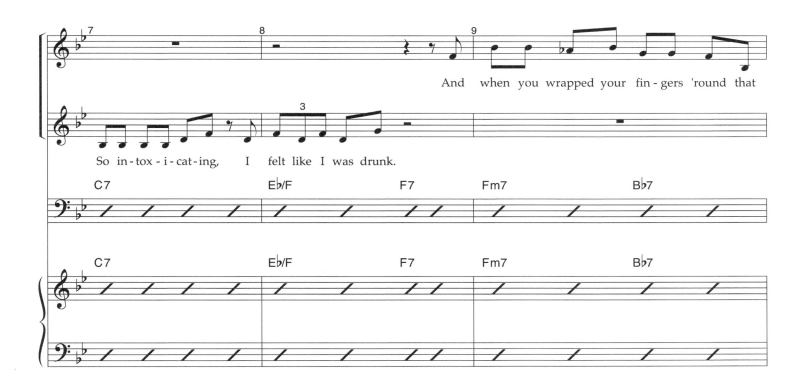

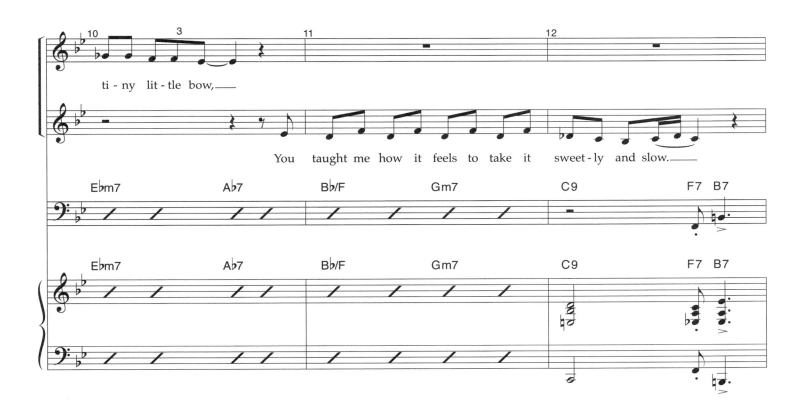

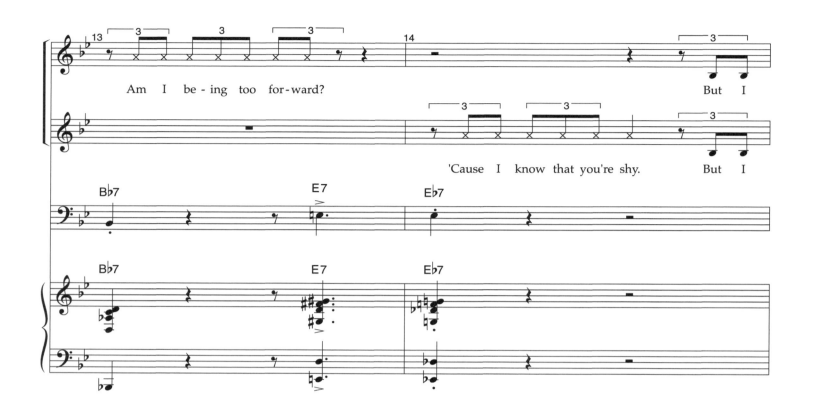

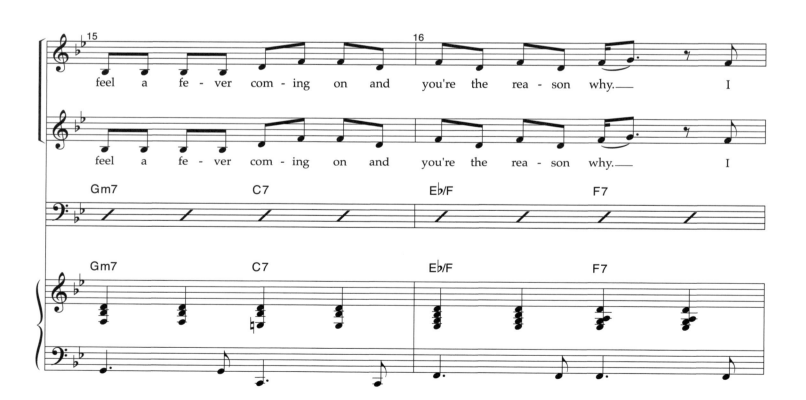

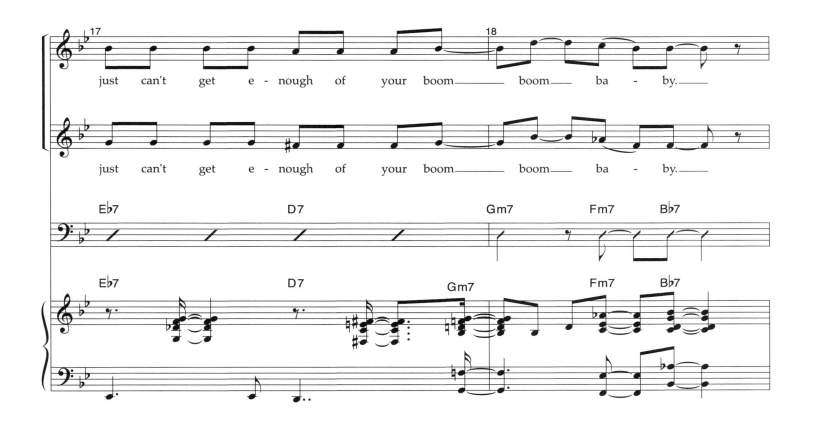

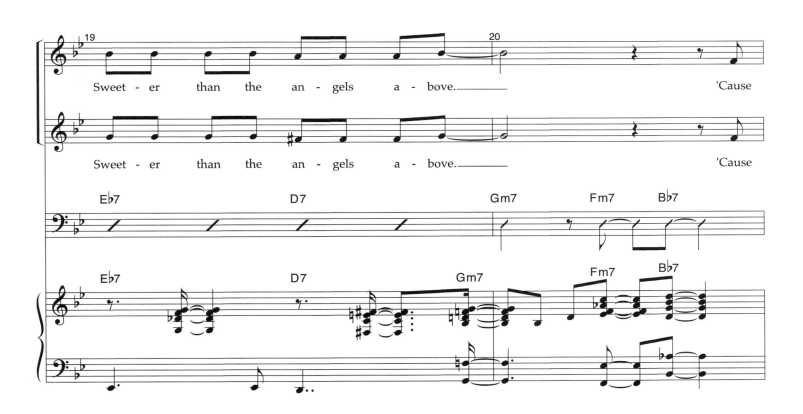

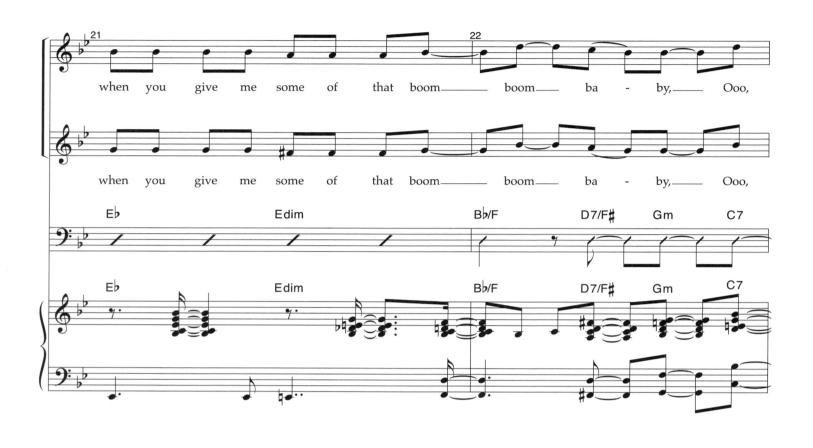

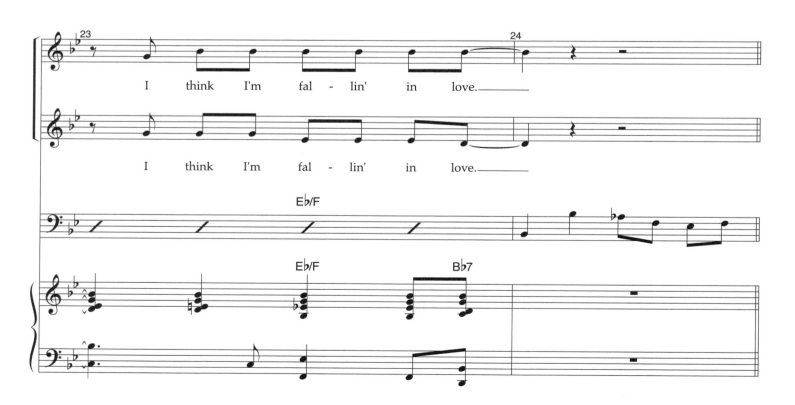

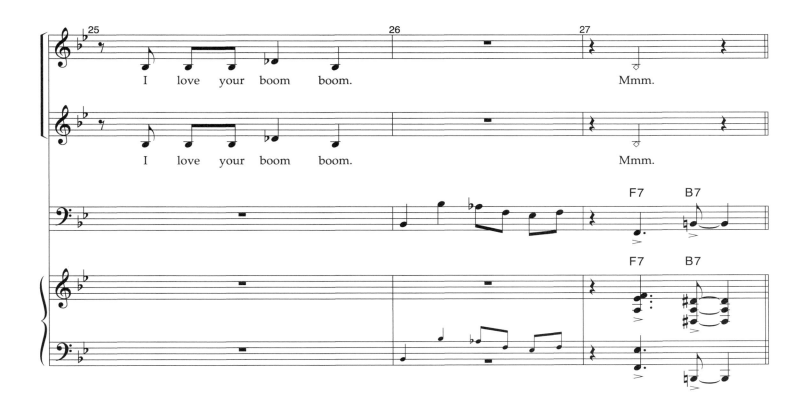

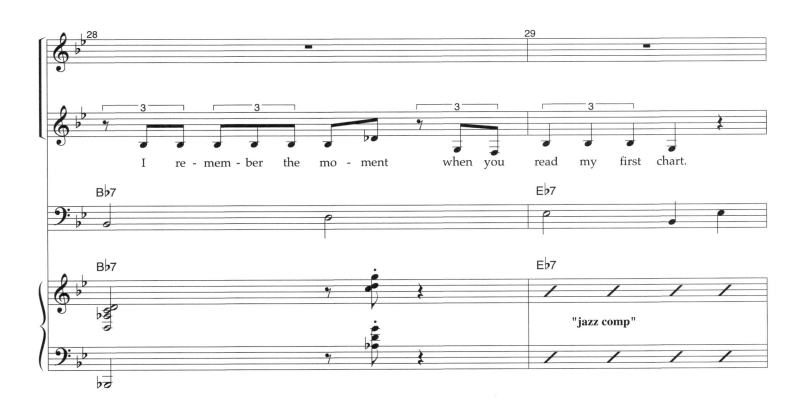

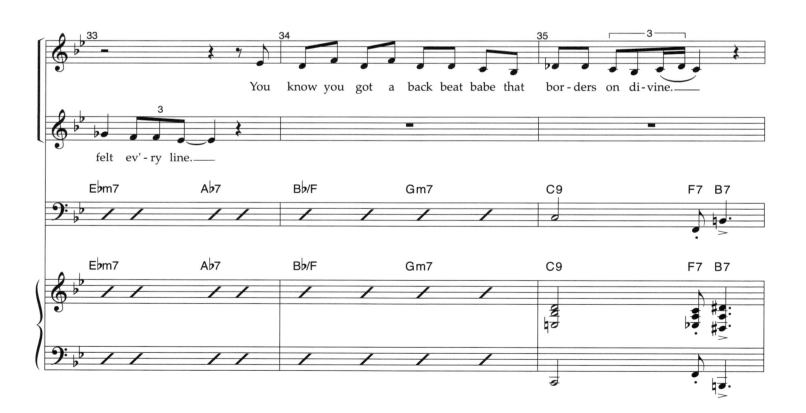

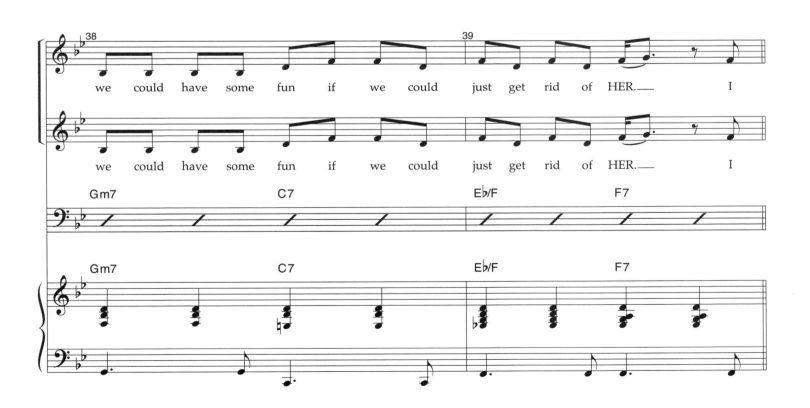

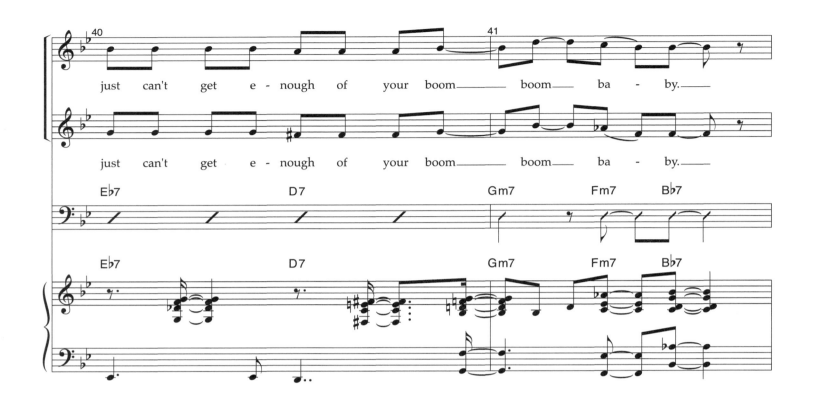

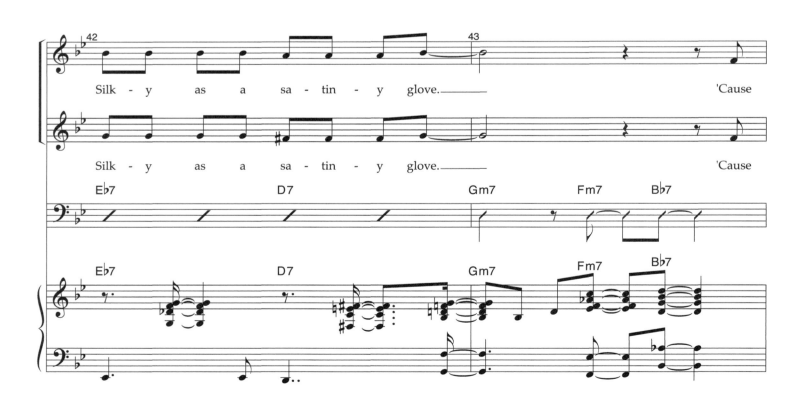

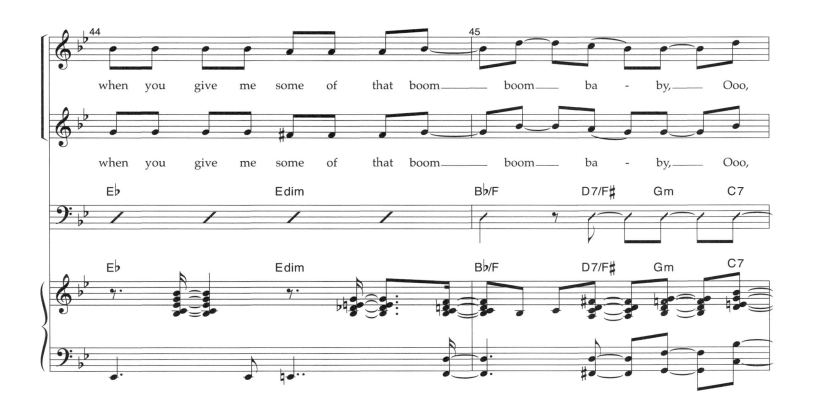

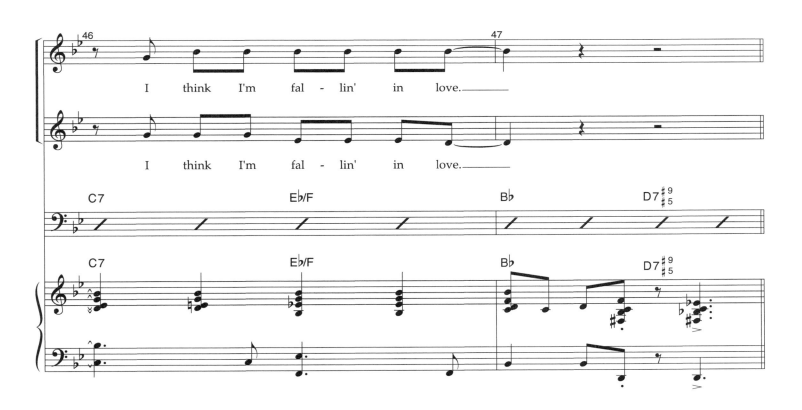

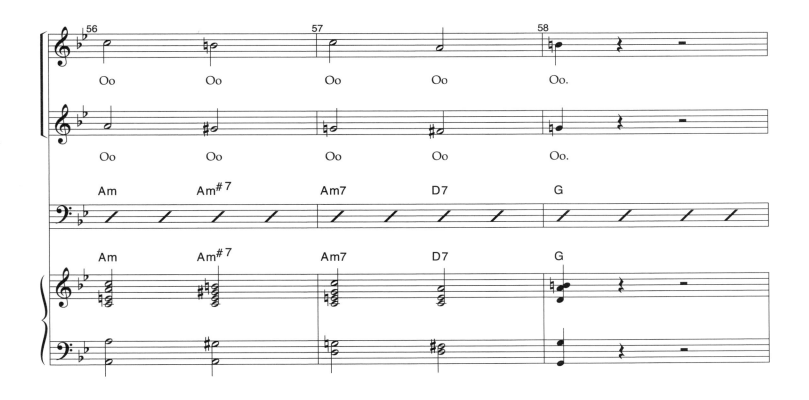

52

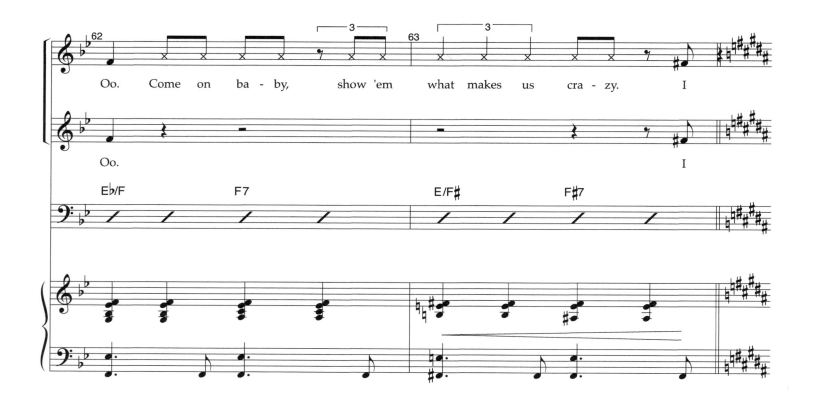

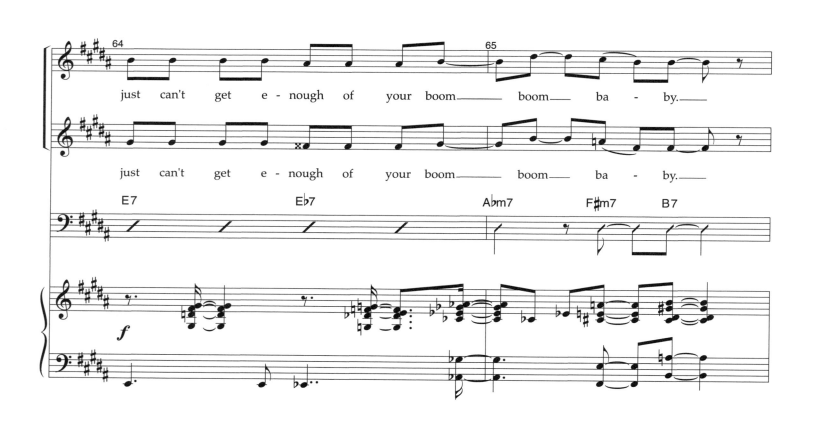

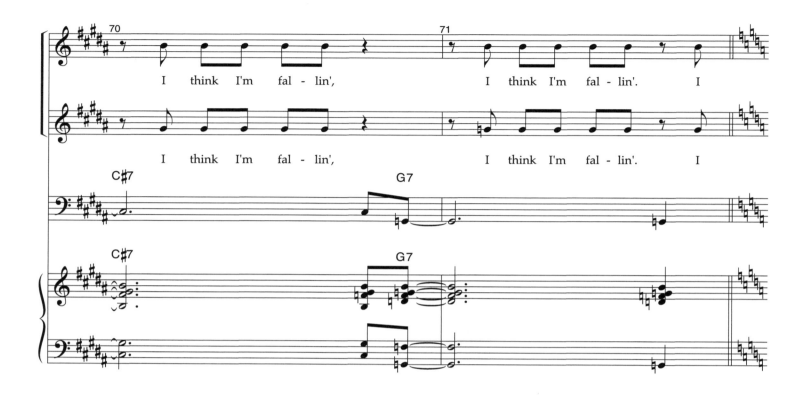

I think I'm fal - lin', I think I'm fal - lin'. I

I think I'm fal - lin', I think I'm fal - lin'. I

just can't get e - nough of your boom boom ba - by,

just can't get e - nough of your boom boom ba - by,

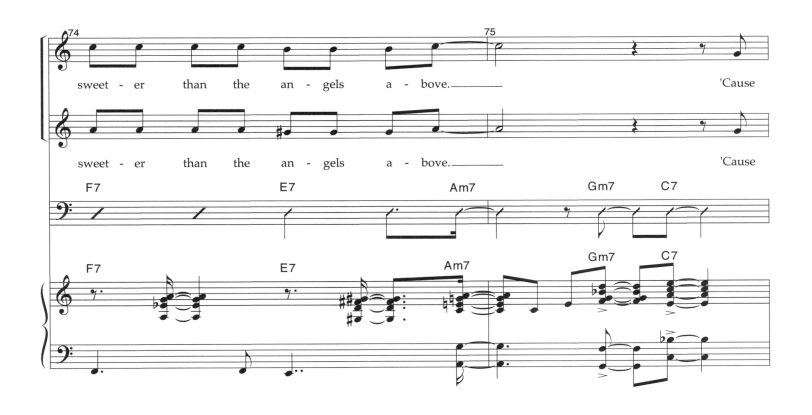

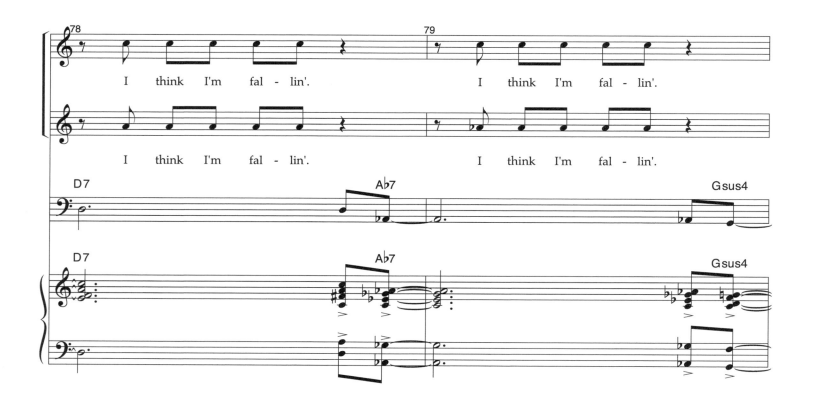

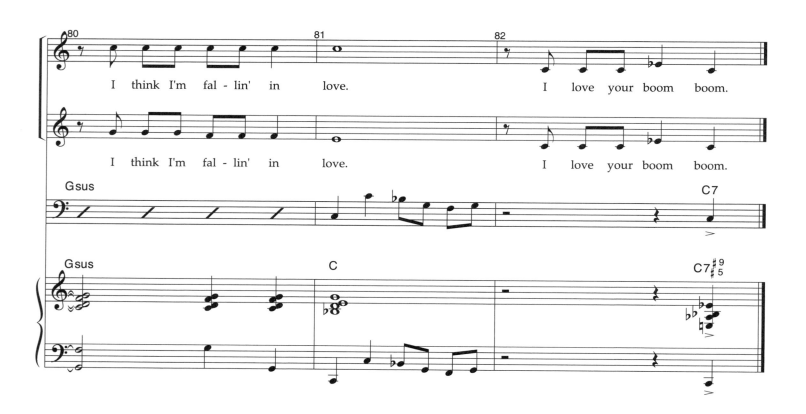

Don't You Be Shakin' Your Faith In Me

Lyrics by
MARCY HEISLER

Music by
ZINA GOLDRICH

58

Faraway

Lyrics by
MARCY HEISLER

Music by
ZINA GOLDRICH

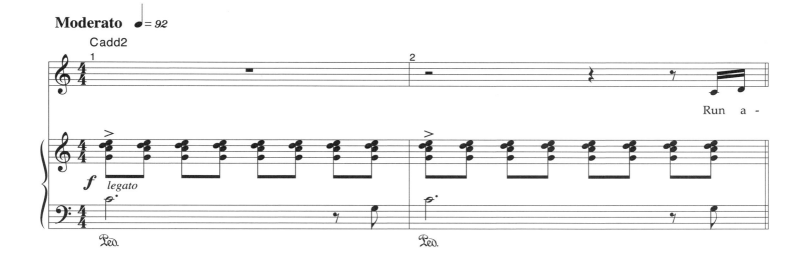

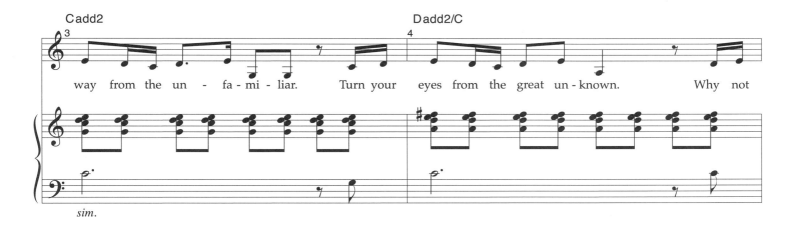

73

Fifteen Pounds
(Away From My Love)

Lyrics by
MARCY HEISLER

Music by
ZINA GOLDRICH

Rock 'n' Roll ♩ = 128

(Spoken) When you're single in New York for a...how shall I say...a long time, you tend to hear the most amazing...

and interesting lines from perspective suitors. I thought I had heard everything, until I met a man who told me this: You've

got the most beau-ti-ful eyes I've e-ver seen.

83

84

Funny How The Love Gets In The Way

Lyrics by
MARCY HEISLER

Music by
ZINA GOLDRICH

88

Hola, Lola!

From "Dear Edwina"

Lyrics by
MARCY HEISLER

Music by
ZINA GOLDRICH

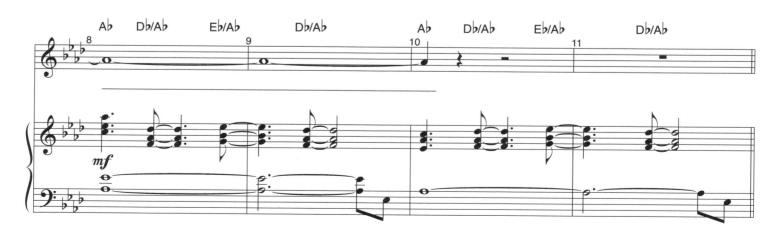

98

102

How I Love You

Lyrics by
MARCY HEISLER

Music by
ZINA GOLDRICH

I Want Them... (Bald)

Lyrics by
MARCY HEISLER

Music by
ZINA GOLDRICH

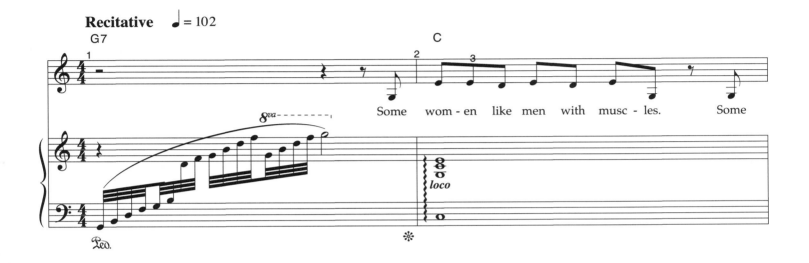

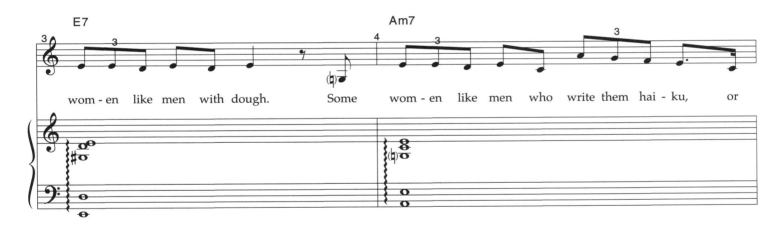

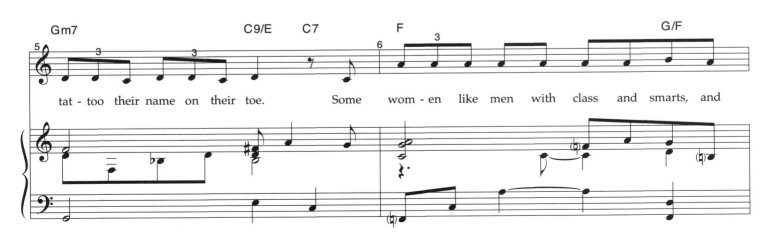

what makes me cra - zy is a lack - of - lock star.

Bald, *(She likes them bald) shin - ing, bril - liant - ly

bald; (bril - liant - ly bald...) flow - ing curls are

so pas - sé,___ tell your Rom - e - o to throw the comb a - way. How I

* (Backup vocals are optional)

The Last Song

Lyrics by
MARCY HEISLER

Music by
ZINA GOLDRICH

119

door-man is mov-ing a - way. It's back to A-thens for Spi-ros, next week he will

fly. How I hate to see him go and I thought that you should

know... in case you want to stop and say good - bye. Say good -

bye. Say good - bye Say good-bye Say good - bye Say good-bye!

124

No "if and or but"._____ This is the

last verse of the last tag of the last song..._____

(not willing to let go of last note)

(running out of air)

What?

Let Me Grow Old

Lyrics by
MARCY HEISLER

Music by
ZINA GOLDRICH

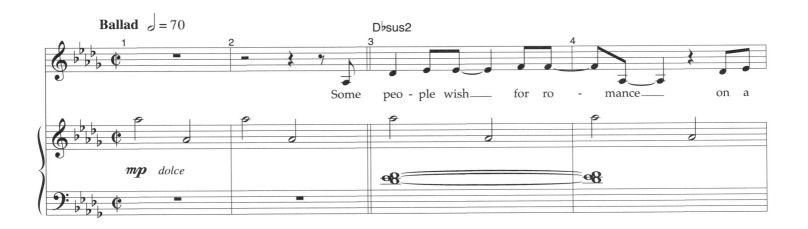

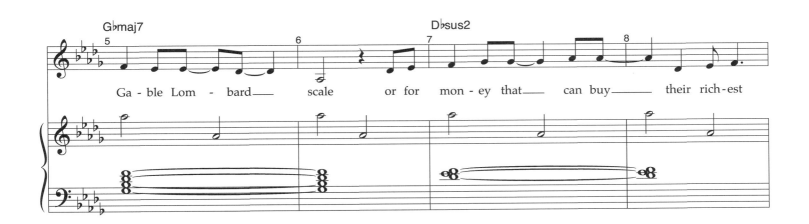

Love Like Breathing

Lyrics by
MARCY HEISLER

Music by
ZINA GOLDRICH

138

139

142

Make Your Own Party

Lyrics by
MARCY HEISLER

Music by
ZINA GOLDRICH

146

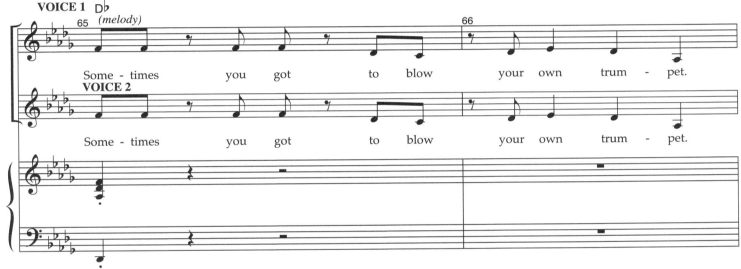

Menemsha Moon

Lyrics by
MARCY HEISLER

Music by
ZINA GOLDRICH

162

The Morning After
(Leave)

Lyrics by
MARCY HEISLER

Music by
ZINA GOLDRICH

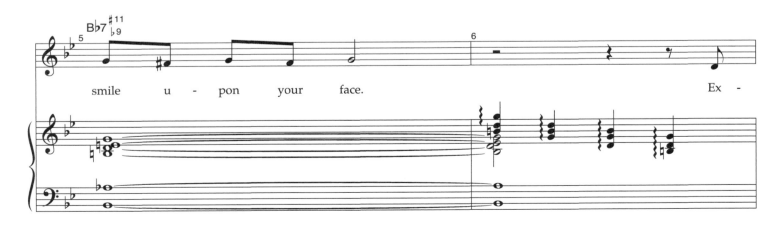

167

168

170

174

Music of Your Life

Lyrics by
MARCY HEISLER

Music by
ZINA GOLDRICH

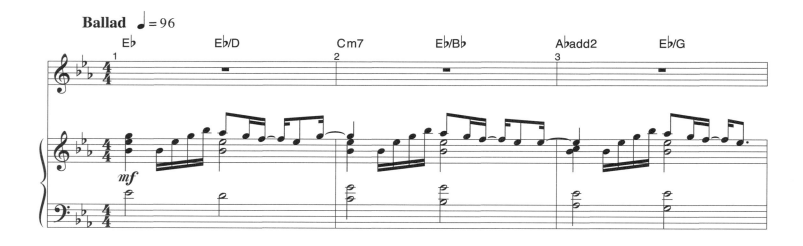

There's a part of me___ that wants___ to be___ a cri-ti-cal___ suc-cess.___ There's a

part of me___ that does - n't want___ to risk___ it. There's a

179

181

I want to make mu-sic. I want to make mo-ney. I want to make___ love.___

185

Now That I Know

Lyrics by
MARCY HEISLER

Music by
ZINA GOLDRICH

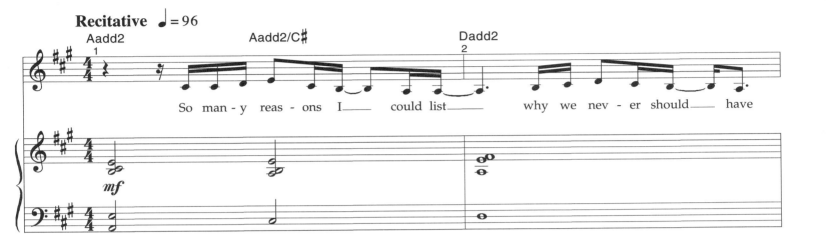

So man-y reas-ons I could list why we nev-er should have

kissed, and a lot of them are good. We're not at all what each oth-er needs

and we both know where this road leads. You point-ed out, I un-der-

Oh, How I Loved You

Lyrics by
MARCY HEISLER

Music by
ZINA GOLDRICH

Oh My Soul

Lyrics by
MARCY HEISLER

Music by
ZINA GOLDRICH

213

Out of Love

Lyrics by
MARCY HEISLER

Music by
ZINA GOLDRICH

217

219

221

Over The Moon

Lyrics by
MARCY HEISLER

Music by
ZINA GOLDRICH

225

227

R. S. V. P.

Lyrics by
MARCY HEISLER

Music by
ZINA GOLDRICH

Sing Your Own Song

Lyrics by
MARCY HEISLER

Music by
ZINA GOLDRICH

243

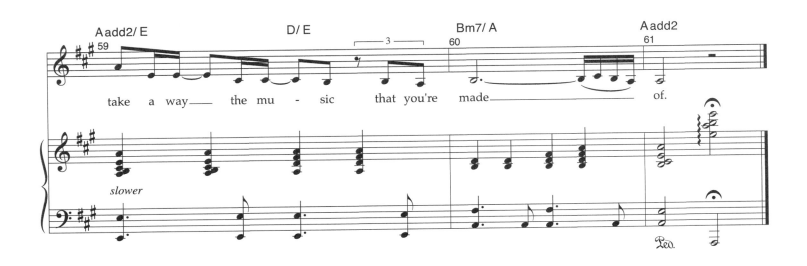

Taking Flight

Lyrics by
MARCY HEISLER

Music by
ZINA GOLDRICH

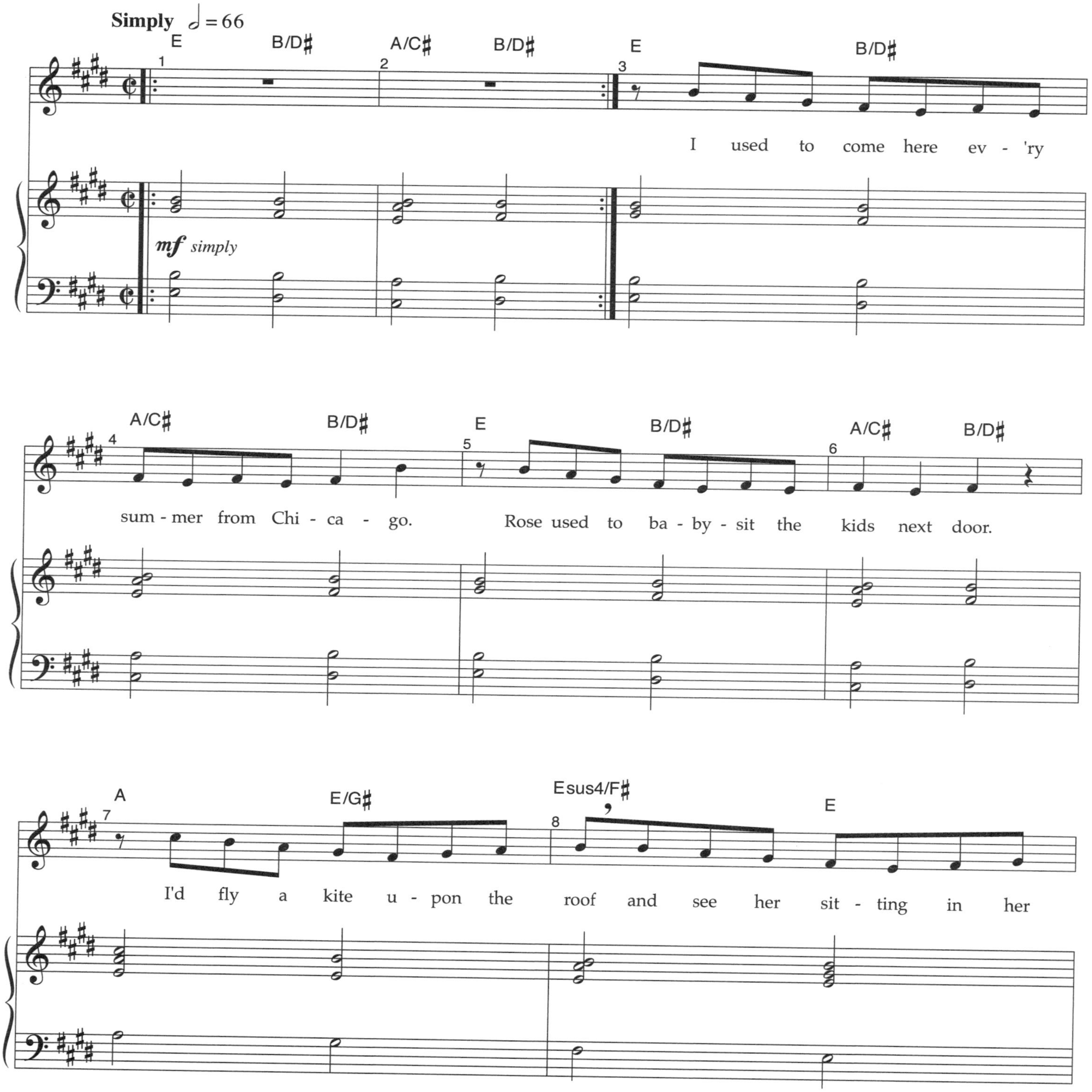

Simply 𝅗𝅥 = 66
E
B/D♯
A/C♯
B/D♯
E
B/D♯
I used to come here ev - 'ry
mf simply
A/C♯
B/D♯
E
B/D♯
A/C♯
B/D♯
sum - mer from Chi - ca - go. Rose used to ba - by - sit the kids next door.
A
E/G♯
Esus4/F♯
E
I'd fly a kite u - pon the roof and see her sit - ting in her

251

pull_____ of the dream that I dream_____ ev - 'ry___ night_____

and the mem - 'ry of love_____

tak - ing flight._____

Taylor, the Latte Boy

Lyrics by
MARCY HEISLER

Music by
ZINA GOLDRICH

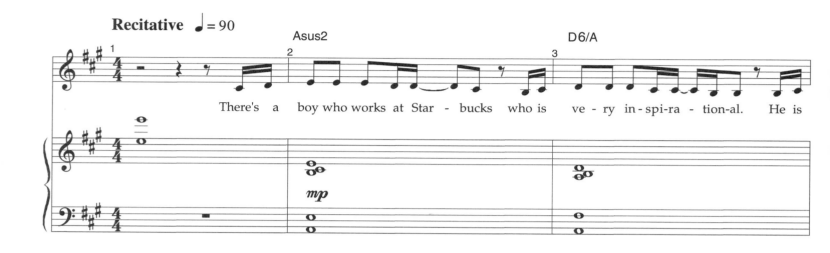

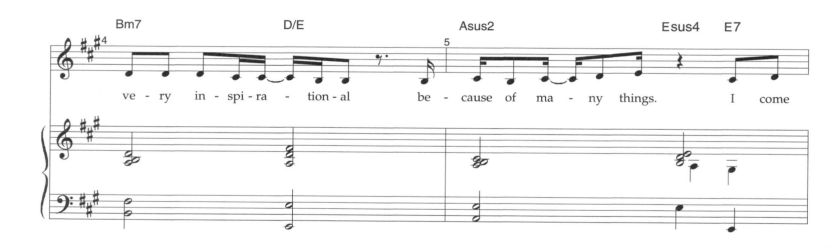

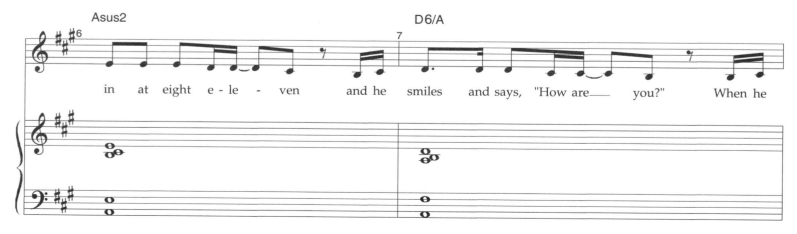

That's All

Lyrics by
MARCY HEISLER

Music by
ZINA GOLDRICH

274

278

There Will Never Be Another Love

Lyrics by
MARCY HEISLER

Music by
ZINA GOLDRICH

289

There's Nothing I Wouldn't Do

Lyrics by
MARCY HEISLER

Music by
ZINA GOLDRICH

ba-by when it comes to____ you, there's no-thing I would-n't do.____

(SHE) I____ would-n't do._____ Oo.____

HE I wan-na wash your

car. I wan-na scram-ble your eggs. Aah._____ Oo._____

What could prove my heart's a-blaze more than go-ing to Mc-Kay's and buy-ing

a - loe ve - ra klee - nex for your nose?

I want to....

Wool - ite your fine wash a - bles!

I wan - na roll your

We Remember Love

Lyrics by
MARCY HEISLER

Music by
ZINA GOLDRICH

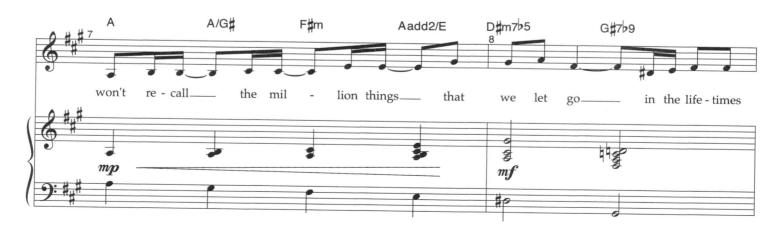

307

Welcome the Rain

Lyrics by
MARCY HEISLER

Music by
ZINA GOLDRICH

When I was a child, I'd run and hide at the smal-lest hint of rain. A sli-ver of grey in the clouds, I'd be un-der a chair. The

that's when you see the true beau - ty of life when you learn how to wel-come the—

rain."

Time pas - ses on. I'm no long - er a child and I've learned a thing or two. I've

learned there are wounds that a mo - ther can not kiss a - way. And